T0287876

MORE PRAISE FOR
LIKE SUGAR

"Roberto F. Santiago's *Like Sugar* is a performative cascade roiling with wisdom. As a child, the speaker is obsessed with the beauty of sadness, imagines that the ceiling fan is a cameraman whose lens records the 'big movie moment / where I would burst into song. Something in Spanish. / Something dramatic about being a woman scorned / like my Tías and Tía's Tías before them.' In the same poem comes the wisdom: 'The problem with losing something you love is not the without / it is the moment you realize you will survive without.' These are poems of survival-as-verb in a life lush with adventure and heartache. One of the survival strategies is visceral comedy, as in a poem which includes the simile which becomes the book's title, as well as recipes for cocktails. He writes, 'he wanted to fuck me, but I wouldn't, so I fucked him / raw like sugar wants to be while Lisa, my roommate, was out / getting pregnant when she shouldvve been at work at the M&M factory.' My head spins like a big whirly lollipop. Santiago is defiant in the face of conventionalizing writerly advice. 'I also know you're gonna / unsheathe your fine-tipped sharpies / from their Moleskine prisons / and scrape across that first-line, / to make a suggestion for a subtler, / less violent opener,' he writes, letting us know not to bring our tight-assery to the delicious too-too-muchness of all this raw sugar."

Diane Seuss

author of *Four-Legged Girl Four-Legged Girl* (2015), finalist for the 2016 Pulitzer Prize for Poetry, *Still Life with Two Dead Peacocks and a Girl* (2018) finalist for National Book Critics Circle Poetry Award and Los Angeles Times Book Prize in Poetry, *Frank: Sonnets* (2021)

"*Like Sugar* is an apocalyptic ars poetica—an overflow of burning cities—a candied and sonic reflection of rage and longing that has turned back to look at itself despite the threat of turning to stone. To suggest a 'subtle, less violent opener' for Santiago's work would ruin this perpetual night going into dawn. 'Someone needs to be brave enough to be themselves,' says one poem, yet this whole book is a lyrical rebellion that's satisfying to read for that very reason. '[T]he sun saunters to the center and bleaches everything,' *Like Sugar* is an undressed prayer left to its own thrilling devices."

Analicia Sotelo

Author of of *Virgin*, the inaugural winner of the Jake Adam York Prize, selected by Ross Gay for Milkweed Editions (2018) and the chapbook, *Nonstop Godhead*, selected by Rigoberto González for Poetry Society of America

NOMADIC PRESS

OAKLAND

111 FAIRMONT AVENUE
OAKLAND, CA 94611

BROOKLYN

475 KENT AVENUE #302
BROOKLYN, NY 11249

WWW.NOMADICPRESS.ORG

MASTHEAD

FOUNDING PUBLISHER
J. K. FOWLER

ASSOCIATE EDITOR
MICHAELA MULLIN

EDITOR
NATASHA DENNERSTEIN

DESIGN
JEVOHN TYLER NEWSOME

MISSION STATEMENT

Through publications, events, and active community participation, Nomadic Press collectively weaves together platforms for intentionally marginalized voices to take their rightful place within the world of the written and spoken word. Through our limited means, we are simply attempting to help right the centuries' old violence and silencing that should never have occurred in the first place and build alliances and community partnerships with others who share a collective vision for a future far better than today.

INVITATIONS

Nomadic Press wholeheartedly accepts invitations to read your work during our open reading period every year. To learn more or to extend an invitation, please visit: www.nomadicpress.org/invitations

DISTRIBUTION

Orders by teachers, libraries, trade bookstores, or wholesalers:

Nomadic Press Distribution
orders@nomadicpress.org
(510) 500-5162

Small Press Distribution
spd@spdbooks.org
(510) 524-1668 / (800) 869-7553

Like Sugar
© 2021 by Roberto F. Santiago

This book was made possible by a loving community of chosen family and friends, old and new.

For author questions or to book a reading at your bookstore, university/school, or alternative establishment, please send an email to info@nomadicpress.org.

Cover art by Alexander Hernandez

Published by Nomadic Press, 111 Fairmount Avenue, Oakland, California 94611

First printing, 2021
Second printing, 2022

Library of Congress Cataloging-in-Publication Data

Title: *Like Sugar*
p. cm.
Summary: *Like Sugar* is a mixtape launched from the frontlines of growing up queer and Puerto Rican in a world where straightness and whiteness embed the very language we speak. These exquisite poems reference pop culture and classic literature equally and lavishly. Cardi B and David Wojnarowicz do the shimmy through this book, as do Nina Simone and Arthur Rimbaud in a torrent of culture, camp, theatricality, and sass.

[1. Poetry. 2. Latinx. 3. LGBTQIA+. 4. Queer Studies. 5. American General.] I. III. Title.

LIBRARY OF CONGRESS CONTROL NUMBER: 2021945143

ISBN: 9781955239103

LIKE SUGAR

ROBERTO F. SANTIAGO

LIKE SUGAR

ROBERTO F. SANTIAGO

**NOMADIC
PRESS**

FOR MARK. FOR VALÈNCIA. FOR ALWAYS.

contents

foreword
introduction

notes
reading guide

foreword

I stepped onto the poetry scene in the mid-'90s, at a time when there were few published books that spoke to my personal experiences. There were openly queer Chicano and Latino writers and whispered rumors of other gay Nuyorican poets, but they identified as bisexual or chose to remain closeted. Without any formal education, I put myself out there as an artist hoping that others would feel inspired to learn, write, and share.

Years later, I heard Roberto F. Santiago recite poetry at a dingy gay bar in the East Village as part of a PANIC! poetry event. Besides fabulousness, he embodied charisma, conviction and most importantly, genuineness. I approached him after the reading to compliment him on his poem, "Save The Date," which would later be included in his debut collection, *Angel Park*. Today, as I write this foreword to his captivating poetry collection, I share words that I always hoped—and in many ways knew—I would have the chance to write.

In 2011, when El Museo del Barrio asked if I would edit a collection of contemporary Latinx poetry, *Me No Habla With Acento: Contemporary Latino Poetry*, Roberto was definitively on the "must be included" list. By 2015, he had his own published collection and, though there were now a slew of young, talented, fearless, queer Latinx writers, Roberto was at the forefront.

In *Like Sugar*, Roberto F. Santiago's words command the page in a way I can only relate to as a spoken word artist up on a stage. His poetry moves seamlessly through childhood memories, politics, art, song lyrics, love, and reverberates with passion.

His voice is authentic, unrepentantly queer, and, as in his brilliant "Fleur du Mâle," he does not care to metaphor the struggles of people of color as a melted ice cream sandwich on the floor. He'd rather tell it like it is, then step

over it and sashay away. In this affecting collection of poetry, Roberto speaks directly to the reader and crafts beautiful pieces about injustice and loss. He also knows how to keep it sassy as in his flirtatious "Self-Portrait as Boy in Nail Polish"—quintessential Roberto, fusing queerness with culture and two snaps in a circle.

He continues this great and essential tradition of sharing our voices loudly and proudly. Long before there were discussions about diversity, equity and inclusion, or we knew to identify as Latinx, there were poets like Roberto pushing the boundaries of individuality. This collection is important because our histories must continue to be shared for others to understand the differences and appreciate the similarities. Roberto holds a lens and shares his truth in such a prevailing way that will hopefully continue to also inspire others to learn, write, and share. *¡Que siga la tradición!*

Emanuel Xavier

Poet & Activist

introduction

In the wake of my first collection, *Angel Park* (Tincture, 2015), I began writing some of the poems that would become *Like Sugar*. In my early drafts, I remember actively seeking to capture what I was not ready to discuss in my first collection. Honestly, I am not sure I really knew what that meant at that time, but I gave myself the challenge to write against the grain.

At the Sarah Lawrence Summer Seminar in 2015, Gregory Pardlo sat across from a teary-eyed poet that was far more concerned with being a good boy than he ever needed to be. In that meeting Pardlo asked me why I was writing for people that didn't deserve my focus. I cobbled together a reason. Could some of the reasons have been related to attending Catholic school from kindergarten through high school? Mayhaps? Could imposter syndrome have played a role? Most likely. I cleared my throat and put on my best job-interview voice. He listened. Smiled. Nodded. Took a deep breath and offered the following advice, *fuck it!* I heard that loud and clear. Realized that this was the real challenge.

That same summer, Diane Seuss explained in a workshop that *assholes* were far more interesting; in real life and poetry. I started to think more and more about the ways I and the speakers of my poems were not always the hero. At the time, I thought that Seuss' words were giving me permission to write my own stories, however recently I realized that she was living and writing in a way that felt so contagiously genuine I would have been a fool not to listen. Or emulate. Or stan.

After that magic summer, I began to examine in my experiences how I was not always right, or good, or even the lead in stories. *Like Sugar* is a collection of poems that does not seek to turn the speaker(s) into the hero of their own stories. The speakers talk about pain and abuse from all angles.

Sometimes we are the reason we fail and sometimes we are figuring it all out in retrospect. *Like Sugar* is bold and loud and guilty and innocent. Some of the poems are angry and thrash about. Some of them beckon you to lie with them. Some ask forgiveness. Some demand contrition.

Like Sugar discusses failure with a sense of urgency. She is queer AF and SHE SAID what SHE SAID. *Like Sugar* is not afraid to directly address the reader through music, pop culture, pain, and rage. Sometimes you gotta write/speak/live through anger, pain, and perceived failure in order to see how far you have come. In the words of Chaka Khan, *It's like sugar, so sweet / Good enough to eat.*

Roberto F. Santiago

Be in love
that enough
hen all the problems start adding up?**"**

Brandy
Where I Wanna Be

"Says he'll play me like a violin
while he burns.**"**

Sam Sax
Meat

And after it's over, we have both become
nen.
Him for the beating,
and me for taking his beating.**"**

Marcelo Hernandez Castillo
Sugar

Domestic

I watched a man
put his hands
through a woman
breaking each of his
fingers.

They fell to the ground
like goldfish
from a fat,
clear baggie.

I kept my head down,
dragged it 'cross the carpet.
His knuckles burst open
like the first buds in March.

Ragged-pink,
breathing.

I would like to say
that if I was a woman's husband,
I wouldn't do this,

but I am not
so sure. That
is failure.

Shelter-in-Place, March 2020

This planet has survived everything;
it will most certainly survive us. We are
no more innocent than our many failures.

At the beginning, we were sons of
a father's quiet: a paper plane
before the folds.

At the beginning, we were a son of
your father's anger: a knife under
a pillow.

At the beginning, we were daughters of
a father's neon: a bone in the basement
with no explanation.

We will always be
daughters of a father
and his lovely child-wife.

A son, dipthonged and
dithering, of dreams
deferred.

A daughter of two
minds with language

for neither &una lengua sin pelo.

Our brothers, sons of
the same father, only claimed
on taxes. tambien:

Actually, at the same time,
but in a different time zone,
Our mother was not a son of anyone's father, except her own:

beautifully spiteful
like fucking someone's man
to get him to shut up.   Her, too.

Security is a Cockroach

Growing up poor meant plucking security from my cereal
after it was half-eaten.

It meant my tiny security guards banded together,
unfurling their crinkly wings into a blanket, to keep me
warm when Papí went to the white part of town—
armed with a flashlight and his textbooks—
so he could afford that cereal.

All this is true. And I say *it is* because it *is*,
and you I know I'm right because the city
I grew up in belongs to them more than it
ever could the rats, trash, fires, or even the
black splats of gum&glass asleep in the concrete.

A fate worse than coriander, Chinese parsley, or cilantro

It is gruesome to know your body will stop at nothing to be whole again.
It will ooze and grow itself back together. Bones fuse. Tails grow back.
Shells and skins are shed and you are made again. Different.
There is no way not to be.

Según tu punto de vista
    yo soy La Mala
        Vampiresa en tu novela
                La   Gran   Tirana.

When I was a little boy I was obsessed with sadness.
I thought everyone was so beautiful that way.
The way their eyes danced like champagne.
I forced myself to cry as a child by telling myself
that no one would ever love me. Said it like a mantra.
Sometimes in the mirror, but mostly lying on my back
until I felt slow tears pooling in my ears.
I imagined my ceiling fan was a camera man.
I would stare at the lens until I got dizzy.
This swirling was my big movie moment
where I would burst into song. Something in Spanish.
Something dramatic about being a woman scorned

like my Tías and Tía's Tías before them:
               es un gran necio
                    un estúpido
                         engreído
                              egoísta y caprichoso
                                   un payaso vanidoso
As I grew into my looks, I did not have to fake these songs
I became my Tías and sung them with as much fire as before,
but I didn't have to coax the tears. I learned that men would love me
as much as I could hurt. El viento y viejito piano'd from pushed earth
and the insides of carved words. Enough of them to keep me here with you
like a monument. Longer than I should have ever been. But when I am gone,
speak of me as if I am still here. It is the very least you can do. Do not force my body
onto another plane so you can sleep as rabbits dumb with smoke. I cannot bear to live
the rest of my life inside a hole,
a cast of a body,   *a was,*   an ever,   and all the ways love can feel.

The problem with losing something you love is not the without
it is the moment you realize you will survive without.
There are few ways to die from that realization
because your body is built to break.

Right of Way

When I was eleven, a blue&white cruiser hopped the curb onto the Grand Concourse.
There were no sirens. It was a getaway.

When I was eleven, I was the victim of a hit&run. An omission of
guilt. The consequences of being the brown son of a brown mom in the South Bronx.

Fled like a teen father is taught, or a quitter is known, or something lesser: an inanimate,
small pain ordinary like the inevitability of.

Standing at that crosswalk I waited for the red to green.
There was more silence than there was anything,

I sometimes remember the impact, the speed, the welling of my eyes,
but most of all the left handlebar welded into my upper thigh.

I had the right of way.
I had just gotten that bike.
It was shiny and blue and fast.
I didn't ride much after that afternoon.
Not for a couple of years.
I was convinced I forgot. But I didn't.
My uncle taught me off training wheels in front of our building.
I remember it and him.
My Uncle died last year.
But he had been dead for many years prior.

One time, in his bedroom, he held a gold bullet.
Small, but heavy in his left hand.
He painted the name of a woman that never loved him back on it
with a bottle of white nail polish she left behind.
That night he called for his mother and I in the other room
and she and I entered his smoke cloud of a room.
He showed us the bullet and its vowels still wet
from cursive. We watched him load her name   into the pistol.
The same one he kept under his pillow.
The same one he holstered at his hip when he was a detective.
He raised the name to his temple.   Smiled.   I heard   the name   whiz throug
him like a case of cheap beer.   He lived.   Sort of.

Sometimes I sit in my tub and stare
at that honch of loose meat and bone.
Can't find my bikescar, but I know
it's as there as anything that ever was.
Deep beneath the iodine. I know it is.
Deep as sin whenever a cop whizzes by me.
Or one gets desk duty for proving ACAB.
Or whenever I'm being told what to do by a man in dark blue pants.

Oakland, after the 2016 Election

The crowd was black-red   &
orange-brown   &
brown-yellow   &
silver-green   &
gold-blue as indigo   &
violent as violets   &
aggressive as the first time you
hear a rap song   without the bleeps.
Some people were queer as
fuck. Some were not. Some were
Black, others were not. Many were
not from here, some were
undocumented. Many were
not. Some might have been,
but they kept that shit quiet.
I saw a white man in a cape
          and a white man in khakis.
I saw a white man with a sign
          he printed on bright white paper
White Silence = Violence.
That night, I wore a sweater with two kittens
floating through space in solidarity with everyone
that has been forced to grab back. In this beautiful nightmare
of limbs and voices thrusting towards the helicopters above
they refused to let us pass. Some people said fuck
over and over.

Fuck the
new leader.
Fuck the
police. Fuck
the Election.
Fuck the
3rd Party.
The uniforms did not
budge. Would not allow us
to pass. They warned us. We
shouted. They warned us. We
warned them back. Music. Megaphones. Shouting. Megaphones. They stopped
warning us. They aimed. The first time you feel the launch of tear gas into a crowd
is like making love to a subwoofer at a house party. It is in you
and through you all at once. Your esophagus is full and twisted.
The ancestors in all their infinite wisdom neglected to mention
the feeling of being choked
by strangers from within.
I thank them for this.
Had they warned me, I may have not heeded them.
Or worse, I would have never felt their hands pulling me up to fight another day.

without causing permanent injury
Oakland, November 9, 2016

I still feel it in my chest
plodding my lungs,
another fog about the Bay.

I feel it when my upstairs neighbor drags a chair across his kitchen.
I feel it when BART is overstuffed and someone coughs
or after one-too-many.

Stun grenade—a non-deadly solution.
Flash bang—an ordinary pain harnessed by the British in the `60's.
Sound bomb—without causing permanent injury.

The purpose of a non-lethal explosive:
temporarily disorient an enemy. Separate them
from their senses A blinding light; an intense loud > 170 db.

Let there be light and flashes of sound,
                    of Orwell dressed blue and black,
                    of us's and of them's.

To temporarily disorient   an enemy. We were
protesting. A right   as American as Black Friday,
as corn-bread stuffing, student debt or addiction.

Out of anger I wanted to smack that flash right back
to ricochet the sun stupid as a gun glistening beneath
the same blue the sea envies of the sky.

Out of fear I ran
from the bang
       from the bursting star
              from the hole they tore black.

Out of fear I thought about going without
Of going to bed hungry. Of how often I would. Had.
Of baby's breath and aerophytes dangling from glass rain droplets.

Of fear. Of hope. Of something that no longer exists.
Of ends and their meetings. Of shadow and escape. Of flesh and war.
Of anything I ever wanted. Of the many ways I've been loved. Of one day being human
    again.

Commute,
Monday Morning

His eyes—milky as morning—
rattled about his skull.

Adam's Apple cold-pressed to clavicle, his face was blank
as a customer-copy.

The train car was steam-thick with bodies.
His suit was grey and itchy rubbing against strangers.

Torso to cinch, both knees to the ground,
he fell.

A tiny Asian woman drops her pink box of donuts
to catch him in full Pietà.

She gathered him at his hips,
cupping his spine.

As he came to, he told her it was:
lack of sleep, a newborn, the heat.

He smiled and explained he skipped the most important meal of the day.
Never drank enough water.

> *I'm fine,*
> *really.*
> *Thank you.*

Life in Gomorrah

At one time, Lot's wife and I were best friends.
We would walk for miles without shoes, building
sandcastles between our toes and naming stars.

A rebel in her bones, I called her Edie
the Stone. She never took no for an answer.
She was brash. Edie hated that I called her *the Stone*.
Every time I said it, she would roll her eyes.

Whenever she spoke, she tore the air
invoking auroras to plash and surge
in her wake.

Edie loved Lot as much as a wife like her could.
She asked too many questions, she often took No
as a challenge. She walked with her head towards
the sun. Edie stared through the sun. Never away.

On the evening when it all was to happen,
she shared the warning with me. Escape.
Forward. I should've remained. Edie saved me
from the brim and smite; stone and flame

and everything else the writers added for color.
They painted Lot a hero, his wife with no name
but "looked back" and "pillar" and "salt." I was behind her.

Watch me catch fire | with both hands
after David Wojnarowicz

He was a glass of spume salty as the Caribbean in June and I
        worshipped him as the Summer.
Summer knows burning's the only way out, so
        several times a year we took turns being Summer.
We stoked each other lithe as wildfires. On some nights, I was
        clever enough to spread across his back On other nights, he was
clever and I was an altar on all fours.There is a science to going up in flames
Or an art
    Or denial
Like the morning after
I gave him love and with it
he built fire.
We watched it neon, singe, and brown pretending to be gods slip ping
        tiny blades back   and forth with our tongues.

Whenever I start to miss him, I remember the mess.
The mess we left behind.
The mess after a roman candle   r o m a n c a n d l e s
A body's rejection of its own has always terrified me
        especially, now as you read this.
We are people   of the body Christlike   in only *that* way
        people of blood and salt and bile.
We are the salt left after the hogs have trampled our garden and the pollen stains everything
        the center of a peach after the pit is coerced from its dignity
        the shaping of beef into discs and the seasonings and blood left beneath your nails

things that sound alike are not
                alike   a body arched no
not arched   slungover vetiver
                a body not slung   or slug
but more accurately split   no
                        not exactly slit into or splat out of
but but t e r f l o w n.

Allow me to address the devil   There is so much I must tell you   not want   must   I do
like pretty   Pretty is decorative   Doesn't ask enough of an audience   Less of a read
Such unnecessary ornamentation is not a challenge and I am unwilling to give into that
Pretty is   a hand inside of me
                why i'll end up red as wanting
                steady as I stuck my fingers between
                the fingers of his crisp and he taught me this
                is what rape feels like.

Take It Like a Man

We've been apocalypsing for years
the slicked shins on rubber prophets
the ghosts and second comings
the brimstone, the martyred,
the Covens and covenants.

I am temptress
thick-clad in leather
call me sugar or
something like a knotted, red, cotton yoke
whip-taut around the neck.

Each lung a-pucker at the edges
tucked inside your chest
like two Harlems
ready to renaissance.
The city-slick outside

tinseled and bled from
a single bulb swinging above
counting the rise and fall of our chests
as I dash bare on its black
lassoed by the teasing of dogs.

Crushed by the weight of sweat
and palms. I pull the rope tauter.
Each rib is bent into lace.
Every open fist, an amulet. Your eyes are stones
skipping over a muddy lake.

I am Little Astrolabe, burning sage to fill a room
bruised by hand & licked with salt.
because you will die soon.
But not tonight,
much too cold tonight.

National Winter Garden Song

Self-portrait as Satan eating macarons, but calling `em macaroons.

Self-portrait as Sharon Olds writing cunt over &over again in a notebook.

Self-portrait as that notebook.

Self-portrait as now. And when I say now, I mean right now.

Self-portrait as a sequence of lily-white, gutter-lilies.

Self-portrait as small metal bowl of sweaty apples.

Self-portrait as skull that may, or may not, be human.

Self-portrait in velvet, crushed blackward to blue.

Self-portrait of a naked man reading Hart Crane's Voyages III.

Self-portrait as I blow him, though I'm not really into it.

Self-portrait as him enjoying me, not enjoying it.

Self-portrait covered in the sweat of two men.

Self-portrait as roiling shades of dark.

Self-portrait as boy too afraid to say anything.

Self-portrait as I had it coming.

Self-portrait as God's wrath, or plague.

Self-portrait as I was, or still am.

Self-portrait in lavender and blonde.

Self-portrait as man, or woman, or not.

Self-portrait in turquoise, as someone I don't want to be.

Jamie & Johnny & Jimmy & Jack

When I am at the bar, I need room to move, but more
        than that I need whiskey.
I need it raw. Not chilled. Uncut. No ice. Never do I
        shoot it. I hold it—orange
as gold—under the eyes they flicker & I strobe;
        holding them closely, respectful
as a pyromaniac, or a captive that lived for so many years
        under the thumb of a love
they've forgotten what life was
        before the pangs.
When I am at the bar,
        I need a sturdy glass.
Any bar that shots in plastic is
        one to close not soon enough &
I will not spend more than a song's time there. I long for
        the swirl about a thick, thick glass.
The way the smoke slides a leg towards the lip
        & slinks back down.
The way a cool girl fingers her bubble gum
        only to chew you back in. Wrist flick
& just like that, I pull that prism to my face,
        lap a catstongue of it. Don't swallow.
I let the music slow to breath-speed & soak in
        what is about to happen. A sting
that sets the roof ablaze. I hold it, teething
        the ridges of my palate to firebloom

soft as smalltalk in lilac & when I can't take it any more
        I let them in. All at once.
To feel finer, free, high-modern & more like an orchid,
        among succulents. Soft as
          moss & gossip I can't wait to share.

accomplice

I worry   that one day   one drink will be the one
that smashes through   the frame,   splits it open grain
for grain   & exposes me   for the animal I've become.

Sifting between   a rerun   of *Friends*   and dinner, I will
find drops of myself   spilled into the empty   of whatever
spirit was on sale. Flashing red   and screaming white

lights will siren and thrash about the knotty pine.
Clumsy, rubber-men with tanks, will jump off trucks,
leap up my narrow stairwell like squirrels to tear through.

Wishing they'd just let me be, as the rhythm of the ram
batters its head bloody   through the door,   I will gather
every piece of broken glass and prescription M&M nestled

in the carpet, under the comforter, in pillowcases, and behind
the armoire into my mouth so that no one will   ever know
I was their accomplice.

As If the First Yes Wasn't Enough

3AM, there's a light
more treasured than
at any other notch
in the morning.

This light splays itself
on the back of a boy
I barely know
& I watch it music at his spine—

an invitation to leap in
(I hesitate), but the light
insists. I wade in it. In him.
He turns and asks,   *am I*   *warm*   *enough, for ya'?*

I skip a stone across him.
Make the light ripple about us
cornflower-soft like my favorite shirt
he will swipe after we are done.

Until the light is no longer, I psalm to him
in his own mouth, warmly for a single now.

Portrait of Petroklos
after Ron Prigat's
"Ken Looking at Caravaggio"

The shadow cast from a single lantern is not biblical,
Though it is indistinguishable in proportion. He is
A symphony exploding slowly at first, in shifts &silently.
A meticulously petalled crescendo, brimming with
Vibration. His breath, a plié stolen from the blackness of
Caravaggio. A merlot-lipped recitation of Cavafy under
Black lace. The black of scriptures that bleed when you touch
Them. Shadowblack as the naked silhouette of an observer on his
Neck. His eyes glister gold-as-riverlight, an expression
Old as the earliest form of wonderment. A pleasury,
A seance, gossamer-white flamelicked and split
Up the center. His vanillin abounds. A furrow roiling
Beneath the mourning psalm of Achilles' horses.
On his brow, a covenant with any creator willing to listen.

A Fire that Started from Nothing

Walking home alone
confused among the chrysanthemums
I shouted aloud: Where do we go from here?
                There needs to be something,
                someplace, somehow far from   here.

Here, where the road is
littered with mottled-black
stones breaking through
or the ones that died trying—
and by trying, I should say fighting—On this particular night,
I dared myself
to think of all
the volcanos
I could've been.
And there are many,
so I implore you: turn   from our cities   as they burn
watch our sky unhinge its jaws like a yawn. Open like a mother's arms
after years without contact. The clouds are your mother's
lips landing upon a swollen bruise violently-violet and hidden away.

Our sky is the color of smoke as it gets in   your eyes. Every so often

the sun saunters to the center   and bleaches everything

pinecones and needles, narratives and evidence of last night   's arrogance

There are many white   gay   men   Orlando,

with many more opinions   about

but this

will happen

again. And then

they will have more to say

but what I want

to say has a memory

of its own   something

they could not

hear   something

like happiness

that violet self

that old, ornery,

original alone.

Grey as the lip

of the lake

where tiny fish
flirt with birds
dancing the impossible-blue.
Those tiny fish were my kin. Mine. With names like the one my father gave me. A name I had

to chase down   to write down   on papers   as they rollicked   reading it   across rivers

agendas and   state-lines   to write this   and only you   will read it.

here

Selfie at a Gift Shop in Old San Juan

You can try on anything
for free. My hands are
ready and open dahlias
facing the new wind and
shimmying. My legs are
long as summer nights
ready to wrap around
your body so you'd take
me with you everywhere.
Here   is a better size
for you. My arms are
songs sung in Arabic
passed down by men
who held one another closely
in times of war. My back is
the curve of a hand-
carved guitar. Its strings only
strummed beside a fire
on a tiny island of singing
frogs and flitting birds with
throats of honey and stories of
long forgotten heroes. My hips are
the dance of two lovers-to-be
full on purple-inked Malbec
and lean cuts of meat fed
by hand. A prelude. The sweetlong

nectar spilled down the chin
to be caught by the tongue
of another man. My lips are
the velvet of a prince
as he climbs down his tower
to tug at a subject under
a trellis cloaked in Blue Moon
Wisteria. The fragrance is—
silent hope and pain—
impatient. My chest is
a low-rider, hydraulic
bounced and waiting
to be taken
for another
spin around
Old Town.
You can try
on anything
for free.

Hackettstown Summer '03

Tommy was a white boy with a fatass, but he couldn't dance.
I loved the way whiskey tasted in his mouth.
His mouth,   a place cigarettes went to die
&he wanted me young
&uncut if I was
young& cut if I wasn't
but most importantly   brown
like sugar should be
he wanted to fuck me, but I wouldn't, so I fucked him
raw like sugar wants to be while Lisa, my roommate, was out
getting pregnant when she should've been at work at the M&M factory:
the one that made sunrises smell like milk chocolate and deer piss.

Lisa was an alchemist
> ~ *PandaBurp*
> - 3 *parts* Vodka [the cheaper|the BETTER]
> - 2 *parts* Sprite
> - 1 *Oreo* as garnish [with the cream floated atop and cookie crumbled about the rim]

and like all alchemists, she always tried to get me drunk
> ~ *#notthefather*
> - *A flute* of Pink Champagne
> - 2 *blue* Pixie Sticks [snorted]
> - 1 *LARGE bite* of a McChicken [with EXTRA mayo]

so one night I might do her like she deserved to be did.
~ *Blaque Jeezus*
- 1 *part* Sambuca
- 3 *parts* Prosecco; 4 if Cava's your thing
- 1 bottle of Windex [sprayed about the room with EVERY sip]

She told me Paulie, her on-again boyfriend, was 6'7"
but not where it counted
& he never went down on her
like I said I would on Kelly.

Kelly looked like Ariel, her skull pushed out a mermaid's red.
She sung like Etta   only without the filth-grit
And I kissed her brows&
jaw&   wrists&   waist&   soft&wet   until I threw up.
Not because she was dirty   or I didn't like it, but
probably because pink champagne and mayonnaise don't gel.
And I didn't want Tommy to find out   and stop dancing.

Fleur du Mâle

Forgive me reader,
I only write the way most people pray.
     When their mother thinks they should.
     Whenever they need something.
     When all else fails.
          To blame someone for everything.
               To be braver than I was in real life.
          To retroactively become the hero of a story. Any Story.
          To highlight my lineage —poetic, or otherwise—
          To be a more authentic version of myself for you,
               but I'm just another asshole pretending
                    my take on darkness and light is more important
                         than the next person's
                              on the next page
                                   of a journal nobody reads (unless they're in it)
                                        Add another line to the CV.

Forgive me reader,
I only write to steal, grind, mince, and julienne (much to the chagrin of my mentors).
     to gnaw the leather in a corner like a bad dog.
     to dub and fawn over images and conversations overheard at the farmer's market.
     to make my self something greater than   the sum   of its swollen parts.

Initially, I began the first draft of this poem with:

> In my Jerusalem, there were
> a million men with two million hands.

I hated that couplet. Shook my head in disgust.
But I let those lines simmer in the sludge for another day, and on my way to work
I saw a melted ice cream sandwich on the sidewalk. I immediately thought,

> Gee! This would make a wonderful poem about the hardships young people of color face everyday.

I titled that poem:

> Self-portrait as a Melted Ice Cream Sandwich in the 'hood

The poem was only one line:

> What dick would let good ice cream go to waste?!

Then I thought:

> Oh Gawd!   That.   Is.   Awesome.
> I totally nailed suffering.   And inequity.

In triumph, I hummed a few bars of Suddenly Seymour.
Whispered, *I'm Savvy Dawktah!*
when I bumped into a muscle-bear in scrubs on BART. He smiled.

When I finally got to work, I crossed out everything
and in my reddest pen and scratched across that page:

> Fuck this poem.
> In the ass.
> No spit.

all my life i've been made to feel as if there was something wrong

with me something broken
unfinished / i was /taught to
hold my anger in my two hands / call it prayer
pray it into penance / a secret
something i had to be ashamed of

men taught me: not to cry
                    crying is for women
                              women are less than
                              woman is made for man
                                        to lie with a man as woman meant I was less than

women taught me: faith / to have it
                    faith in no-good men
                    faith en la familia
                    faith i'd get out of / wherever the fuck i was / one day soon
                    faith in a higher power / patient enough / for us / to get it right
                              before our final days

faith taught me: to keep secrets
                    secrets taught me to lie to people
                                                  people i love
                              people i love / leave
                                        too soon / people i love / never knew the trut

owing up &being taught you're broken is corrosive
ourns / deep /
ting away / rust-red / it starts
the wrists / where pulse becomes fist
lled up / like kleenex / sometimes crying is
e only way / to let out the poison / sometimes violence is

owing up / i had to /quickly /
owing up / i had to / raise others
to pedestals / high / higher / & so high
eir rights negated my own
my wrongs carried loftier sentences
worse conditions in schools / parks / hospitals / housing
l they deem our homes fit for their consumption

eping my rage / a secret / made me think i was dirty
ushed it down / hid from myself / from my power
e women / & queer people of color / have been taught
r thinking about rights / &love / &how it feels
love someone down to nothing

on't remember much / about how i wound up / in anger management / but
e counselor told me: i ran after a bigot boy in gymshorts
                            carrying brandishing a hockey stick
                            i explained shouted i couldn't take it any more
                            i launched the puck across the field and smashed through
                            his shitty smirk face
emember   his taunts
               his laugh
                                    his head bouncing off the grass
on't remember raising the stick i don't, but i wish i did

anger management blamed me / for my circumstances
tattooed me weak / dirty / broken
absolved him of his wickedness/ punished me
for my anger / but it never left /
i kept it / because that shit is mine

Bathroom Hyper-ballad

You taste the way I knew you would.

Like texts left on read.

Like being broken up with over voicemail.

Like listening over and over to that message whenever you need to feel like shit.

Like someone I kissed once before, but will never again.

What are you
        so afraid
                of?

Pressed against the wall you look like
the boy on the poster
and you might be him,
or maybe not.

You kiss like you've been waiting
to be taken from loud places.
An open-mouthed slow as silhouette,
a work of art in scorpion tongues afire.

Fire fast enough
to die young,
their tails drag
across my chest.

I reeled you in
whispering something
Björk might shout
off a mountain—bottles, car parts, and cutlery.

A flesh-soaked prosecco, hands&buttons,
tug&loop, fizzing my tongue flooding
my bloodstream. Drink me until I am
no longer here.

Index and middle finger.
An echo. A stain. Sun
in my mouth like breath
through cigarette.

U Up?

In the jet-pitch of night,
I refuse sleep
and its lulling touch.
Were that devilry to swallow me whole,
I'd grip it
by the throat
from the inside.
Each finger
an arachnid of
bent cigarettes
tearing through flesh
to get to a place
where I might gather the means
and materials to march across
another Ooh, baby.
Not tonight. I don't wanna
fuss&fight. I just wanna
make it right, but I'm a fool.
I march towards the dawn,
letting loose bits of light,
So I can retrace my steps
and re-collect them
inside myself for you.
My neck &lips tenderthick
with shine,
a twitch,
a flicker,
a blink

like nebulae imploring
Give me all your love
&don't stop
My love's waiting
when you reach the top
all   night   long
s   p   r   e   a   d   i   n   g
gold-black through purplesmoke.
I will admit to being much less than advertised—
with my filthy hands and red face—
but you only call me when you're lonely
and need some one.
Not me. One.
And I am not going to beg you
to be human   again.
When we're so close to the
Shoo do do do do do do doow
            Shoo do do do do do do doow
and all you want is to get lit
up   and razed
to the dirt. Have no fear
I don't practice what I preach,
I always have fistful
of stones for you
and a pretty glasshouse.
Inside is a loveseat,
suede as starlight,
upholstered moonful
as licorice, blackwet
with nighttimetalk,
like spit in the movies,
but better than that
I gotta big

mouth   and
        an urge to
                back it   up.
So come into my bedroom honey.
                What I got will make you spend money
                        All.   Night.   Long.
And I need it while I'm young &neon enough
to under-appreciate it. And you love it.
Always do. Until I get all Liberal Arts on you
and ask you one too many questions.

Single

Run to the devil and raise your eyes towards the sun while you do it.
These are the new rules of courtship. Find a boy and make him lovely.
Say pretty things and kiss him roughly. Drag a crucifix made of poppies
across his chest. Let it fall apart and spill down his back: black seed, petal, & stamen.
Bite off
        more than
            you can
                chew
                and chew until
                        you swallow
                              because spitting is for quitters
and quitters never get to ride shotgun in an S-Class, or get invited to Palm Springs
for the weekend. Come undone and cast forth your blackest pearls to catch swine in the act
of being swine. Make him love you by changing everything to fit his mother's expectations.
Be an iceberg on the move, searching the world over for his exes and do what they wouldn't
and do it well. Find his fault lines and dance on them naked. Lift your voice with both hands
until the stars rain down   and pretend you had no idea what you were doing. Turn your bod
inside out
        and into a place of worship—full of gold and myrrh.
Bend over
backwards.
Become an altar.
Kiss scripture onto his brow. Inflate his
sense of worth   to the point where
you lose every argument because he can do no wrong. Rinse. Repeat.

The Cavalier Nature of Electricity, or Me, salivating on the floor
after NEEDSUMLUV

Whenever I'm in love, a warm animal-scent lingers—
Sweat &sandalwood, a top-note of copper pans.

The scent is so running-water-electric
I think I might hurt myself, or I am sure of it.

It's not normal &such a pity to be a fool
foolish enough to love a man as I do.

When he's near, I fixate upon the sweetest nothings.
A daydream swelling above him as he lectures.

I devour everything in the way he rests his right-hand
on my left shoulder.

A static j o l t i n g whenever he laughs
&reaches over to rest his hand on my moment of skin,

each moment a moment longer than the last,
but never too long.

Just long enough to prove he is there
&I here.

Amperes &atoms. Fleshy, opposable thumbs
&a current that flows between us, accountable-animals.

Us—in his office—tearing me apart & jing-a-ling
his jewelry. Plain gold ring. Smokeful &exuberant.

The sluice—a current—loose from me,
burning his neck through the collar.

Flesh feels better when it's taken.
When people can see, but pretend they can't.

the time we should have kissed
after Hart Crane

My hand a hand of melted ice   under the constant wonder of your eyes   a past

meticulous but now alone on the cragged argosy of forsythiaflashes forsake your flesh   dearest

poet   drop your pen   crawl to me   through dirt on hand   and knee

tear off your pages and lie   beside me   in the teacupyellow of flowers

I have no name for   Here on this mountain the wind pours wine   in every colour

If you would lie beside a body like yours   a body like mine   we would write verses

inside of each other with twigs and salty teeth   We would be a composite of elselives Softly—

at first—like white lies   And even sooner after much more thunderingly   like the lid of a

piano slamming or the first time I shoved an avocado—rindpitandflesh—down   a disposal with a

fork   or like the sounds of tin-can instruments which is like music but not   music We could make

enough of it to fill the lake behind your voice with warm spit and expletives So dark the waves upon that

lake   Big waves like batterblackened and little waves   like nausealapping over both of us.

Notes on
How to Love Me

If you're gonna love me, you gotta give me Half-Time Show.
Purple Rain. Full-voiced, chesty &rude.
Too black. Too brown.
Too cherry. Too proud.
Too much sky. Too too-much.

I need you to not miss a beat
as the rain burnishes the stage.
Let loose: loud, lilac, &lavender.
Souse them speakers in sparks.
Soak that music to the bone.

I need you like I need you to try.
I don't need success. I need effort.

If you're gonna love me, you gotta be bold.
Bold enough to grab what you want. Bold
enough to hold yourself up. Bold enough
to let me drown. Bold enough to lift me
off the ground when the ground is lava.

I need you to force the air back into my chest, until it turns black
and I loosen the blue
pour it red from both wrists
possessed by Cézanne
creating the illusion of movement.

Once you've said it,
you let it hang there—three days straight
Adderall & Red Bull—midair.
So close to the knives;
serrated and waiting.

I get along without you very well

I hold onto my lovers like fresh-cut flowers
though sometimes I wish I didn't. Full disclosure:
I've been yelling at dandelions, again. Golden-green ghosts,
cold as neon. Capricious little nymphs stealing the sun;
flaunting a yellow yellow-as-margarine with far less conviction.
Why won't they listen and loosen the purple-frosted-pinks
from their electric grips. Damned lion-toothed goblins
pull the mariachi blues as they approach with open-mouths
like a reply to a prodigal lover after midnight.

Yes, I understand, flowers probably don't speak English,
but they appreciate music, so they must understand tone.
Mine's as pointed as a sixth-grade math teacher.
They're just stubborn. Fickle and frightened.
Much like we all are. And after I tear the final petals from their rosette,
I hold onto them like I would hold onto anything—
tightly and in a fist before they are no longer
beautiful. Crazily. Drunkenly. Like someone gazing back at you
from across a table; across an evening; across the better part of a decade.

A poem, like an ex, is never finished

only finished off, admonished, and abandoned at the ellipsis.
A deliciously neon-happy record of us.
A stack of lottery tickets in his mouth.
A portrait of him howling at the Moon,
or tossing my keys out the window.
We made-out on a forest of park benches
until the cicadas stopped their chicanery.
We probably could've kept going,
been brothers, or sons, or love.
Forever celebrating never going home
again.We were home. My first
touch was a torch
to a ramekin. Blue
flame & chapstick.
The second was silver
smashing
a helmet of sugar.
It shouldn't have   happened,
but it redeemed us
from the failure
of the first. The third
was a mouthful. We weren't
ready. Or sober. Or serious.
The fourth was too much.
So it didn't really count.
The fifth took you home.

The sixth licked the bowl
clean. The seventh let you
stay the night. The eight
was after an argument,
you left   in a fit, but
the damage was done.
I went to o far, but this is   what you came for.

Shelter-in-Place, April 2020

I measure the summer distance from you to me
in how long in a day I can go without speaking
to another person—I go for long walks downtown,
visit the markets, read Merrill in a rose garden,
sip tonics of gin-honey, and light incense on the beach.

If you don't count polite nods and tight-lipped smiles,
I can go pretty long, but ˋround midnight I lose count.
Then I draw another bath and contemplate breathing underwater.
This distance from you is not time. It is not poetry.
I feel no comfort in its diction nor closure in its punctuation.

I don't want to be dramatic, but I have a feeling I won't make it
to the other side of this summer. I'm gonna burn. Burn it
down in a tiny blaze of glory. An amateur fireworks display.
Too much sun under the skin. Burned ˋtil I blister and run.
Burned the color of everything. A cleansing burn until

my next breath. We live too long to not be so loved.

Little Wings

Across the creek, a boy will collect his belongings from a picnic blanket.
He will place them into his red-and-black gym bag—full of books
and booze and warm-smelling underclothes.

After months without rain, this creek will become a sea.
More than an altar for little wings and rubber branches.

That day will not be remarkable by any measure.
It will be a faded, well-worn corduroy. A hand-me-down sky,
thick like bacon fat—an oily greige.

The second boy will stand less than an arm's-length from the first.
      He will take several beats to register what he just heard
                  to catch his breath
                  to find a feeling. Any feeling.
And as he does, the sky will fall to the ground
in fragments of sound like mini-bar's worth of glass bottles smashing against a wall
                  or a drawer of silverware spilling onto the kitchen tile.

The wind will judder the surface of the creek
like a cough you try to hold in— a dulcet bass.

The wind will birch the first boy's near-blond curls about his long, sharp face.
      He is lovely in an almost unexpected way.
Another person with his features could not have been assembled so perfectly.
      They would have been all right-angles and sandpaper.

The first boy looks like an Evan, so Evan he shall be.

His cheeks are cream bruised raspberry.
e is lanky in an elegant way. An egret
hioned from pipe cleaners and piano wire.

e second boy looks like the hero in a novela
            but not as a man, as a schoolboy. Before regret. Before potential
only seen in retrospect. His face is soft as olive oil.
            His hair, unmoving in the wind, knows its place. He looks like a child
dier before he knows he is one.

e second boy looks like a Ronaldo, so Ronaldo he shall be.
s arms are too long. His torso, too short. He has the legs of a minotaur
ilt to spar and take on water.
en through his jeans he looks like a kickboxer.

 this very bank, they will
 at each other beneath
ludge-sky.

e billabong will become a river. The crumbling firmament will resurrect
 the mosquitoes that ever lived. The sounds of them hatching from their wintry graves
ll awaken a battalion of blue jeweled dragonflies.

agonflies can lie
rmant for years.
ey thrive on
arning.

e rain, like most good things,
ll only last a few short moments.
hen the sun returns to its rightful place,

the zither of insects will fill the creek.

Evan will apologize as he is wont to do.
Ronaldo will accept, mapping a constellation
with his fingertips from the hairs along Evan's jaw.
The ones he always manages to miss.

And there
in the mire
Ronaldo will undress Evan.

Perhaps it will be the other way around.

A dance
of buttons
and sleeves.

Evan will be so eager,
he won't remove his socks.

Ronaldo will take his
time. There will be nothing, but
gravity on him.

Gravity, near blond, and the wings of a million dragonflies.

Tongue-tied

He was a wide-eyed winter and I, a scarf.
I wanted him to devour my *me* and all that made me
man, or woman, or worthy of skin.

His mouth was the mouth of a million sailors
long gone. The way it hissed as he danced
to the sounds of arrows cutting through sweat.

He kisses me like we are having an affair.
Broken, breathily, like this was the last.
Give him a stage, he'd make butterflies from thunder.

There are flowers in any room he filled.
In a bloom of night, I willed him mine.
Or more likely, the inverse.

To possess him was to be possessed by him.
To house his body inside your own.
On nights apart, I ache for that white fence.

Laying under stars he told me
he was once tongue-tied.
The condition was present at birth.

A short, tight band of tissue tethered his tongue to the floor of his mouth
until he was a little boy standing in front of a mirror
with a pair of cuticle scissors.

He was eleven.

He said it took three nearly imperceptible snips.

Making the hand motion, he said it felt like
                                   being pulled apart by
                                             three thousand bee stings.
He stared into mouth in a mirror.
Swollen and red, he spit into his hands
and felt parts of his mouth he'd never known until that night.

I knew I was falling when I imagined you dying.

I wondered how. Would it be cancer, and if so, which kind?
Or will some monster steal you away while you're sleeping?
Will you suffer? How will I go on without you? How long before
I go on without you? Will there ever be another boy? Will he be even half-as-witty?
Maybe an architect or a lawyer. Maybe an older gentleman with a job-title
he never shares explicitly. When I ask, he'll say 'I work in *advertising*,
or *finance*, or *acquisitions*'. Something really abstract. Something that requires,
NAY, demands he speaks with a pan-Euro accent. Or maybe not.

I knew I was falling when I began to worry there were too many stars.
To conquer this worry, I learned each star's name. Every night I'd call unto them,
one by one, and tell them about you. Eventually, I convinced the foolish orbs to stay with us
forever. I stole each star from the wing, and neck, and hoof of Pegasus.
I saved the three shyest for you, and while you were sleeping,

        I placed Markab under one of your ribs.

        I hid Homan where your wisdom tooth would have been. And finally,

        I massaged Matar at the base of your spine. The space I love most.

I did all this before any gods or mortals could notice the missing stars.
And sooner than they could take them back as quickly as I knew they would.
And before there were none left.

I knew I was falling when

        Birds flyin' high / Fish in the sea.

I sang songs in my head.

        Stars when they shine / Blossom on the tree.

Songs in the key of Nina Simone.

Songs she never had the chance to hear.
Songs like *Uptown Funk*, or *Drunk In Love*, or *Chandelier*.
I knew I was falling when I stared at you reading the paper and I sung each song to you
at the top of my mind's lungs. I knew when I thought you could hear me
silently singing *dragonfly out in the sun…* I knew when I thought you could be singing alo

I knew I was falling when I couldn't stop offering my every opinion regarding everything
I have ever heard the moment I heard it.
Individually wrapped morsels of me.
Like butterscotch or those awful red candies
wrapped to look like strawberries.
The ones that taste nothing like strawberry.
The ones my grandmother kept in a candy dish on her coffee table.
The ones I ate every single time I saw them. As if *this time*, would be *the one* they changed
to raspberries or something even remotely natural.

I knew I was falling when I started to
become more like you in order to
think about the ways you might've
fallen for me. Maybe you would
fall right off that couch.
Smack your little head on the edge of our coffee table.
Spilling baby carrots and tzatziki everywhere.
And you'd get up Moonstruck.
Doing your worst Cher impression.
Or maybe your worst impression
of Olympia Dukakis doing her *best*
impression of an Italian mother—and wife—taken for granted.

I knew I had fallen when I held my breath. For no reason really. Anyone can
hold their breath until they match their lover's breath in bed. Counting seconds
until their exhales eddy into a CO_2 orgy raunchy enough to make a bonsai blush.
I knew I had fallen when I bated my breath in anticipation of nothing really.

Just knowing you would be there to smile, or wink, or wince at me.

I knew when I began to want.
Most people think *wanting* is a sign
               that some *thing* is missing. I disagree.
Wanting is a result of living. Or loving.
I want because my needs are being met and I
have the luxury of breathing steadily enough
so that the world—were it all mine—could be improved upon.
I knew when I wanted so badly, without worry of getting
what I wanted. Something intangible so that I could return
a piece of something undiscovered. Something old.

Maps

He was always a strange boy.
A mirage dancing, flicker and flame,
to bossanova like it was hip-hop.

His bedroom was plastered with maps,
not with feather-haired smiles in swimsuits
or bubblegum-pink pop stars, but with maps.

He spent mouthfuls of time pressing them between
thumb and forefinger, studying the routes he could have taken
and the ones he had been taught to follow.

Laying them atop one another,
he drew new trails in different colours
for future adventures and strange boys like him.

Years later, he found himself alone on a city street,
dressed in another language. His footsteps tracing the river
he once knew as soft-blue ink on his favorite map;

where he wrote 'home' across it in cursive.
This swirling arch connected the banks.
The arch, a bridge, a fingernail width, united two rivered cities.

This river traveled between bones and cliffs, snaking through
veins of iron and glass. His river ran freely within the borders
of his words. The strange boy was a cartographer, a geographic artist
in the directions of hands, mountains, and shades of green.

He taught me I was
a compass. I taught him
maps have no sky.

You, Therefore
after Reginald Shepherd

When I try to remember myself
before there was you, I stand between
orbits of memory too distant to reach.
And in the time it took to surrender,
I have never been more free.
It is in the seconds that burn away,
razing me up just enough to pull you
down into—and onto—my loss
of breath. I belong wherever you are,
and hope, and dream. I give you shelter within
my trappings of skin and synapse.
All the while proclaiming you to be the sole heir
to my oscillating limbs.
Each of your words sakura still
to the rise and fall of my chest
when you finally see me
seeing you from the distance of arms.
May our story catch fire amongst limb
and freckle, and hair and bone. Burn
ember, and writhe into whatever water
whispers wet. To quiet whim and will
in favor of wanton want in every sense
we acquiesce and evanesce the evidence
ever since the very first days we ever spent togethernight forevermore.

Leave

My wicked love strums a guitar, knuckles bloody like an animal.
My love sleeps in bursts. Bubbling slowly like bad thoughts
filling his glass on a nightstand.

Whenever he was close enough to burn, I'd find any reason to strike him
with all my fires choked into a closed fist. For all the times I bit my tongue
purple and my mouth filled with copper.

The mouth where hurt travels
slow and we often took turns
being unavailable.

I often thought of ending it. Leaving with my tiny scars in a tote bag.
But I enjoyed the sharp of his teeth tearing a bit of skin from me
A talisman, for him to keep and digest and never forget.

To Be Safe With Him Again Possibly, Maybe

If everything that ever lived forever lives in a single line of poetry, then therein we will
also find nothing.   We all think we are the hero of the story. We aren't. We can't all be
          the good guy.
Someone needs to be brave enough to be themselves. I know I wasn't always
the cavalry   and he needs me now like he needs another hole in his head
or more debt   or another song about getting over another no good,
          down-right rotten man.

Maybe it's the new drugs, or the dead-end job or the same ol' thoughts creeping in
during the come down like nausea, or hiccups, or my old life full of promises
bolted shut. Promises are best for the keeping, so save them.
Sprinkle them lightly with flour. Wrap them neatly, in unbleached parchment.
Tie a pretty bow in twine around the wrapping. Stick them in the leftmost corner of
the icebox.
          Obviously,   save room for the ham steaks, but do not use chicken
                    eggs, nor should you
          use quail, but duck,   maybe turkey.

And in that fever-scarlet recipe there will also be a shiver of another day. Good enough
to waste
some time. Another silly smile glinting with emerald light
over light refreshments. Have another
black sugar   and you
grey salt   and me
pink sand   and them on the other side of happyconfused.

I've always said: saying I'm sorry
and saying I apologize
aren't the same thing.

Feathers Falling

from the palm of my hand
nightful as a coyote
under the weight of
a lesson unlearned

did you love me   bitterly?
bitter as I am sweet   bitter as I was
                        made to be
                        &dream, but never was?

For—what would have been—our anniversary, I celebrated
without you. I let gin whiskey &vodka blossom from my lips
all across our city. I avoided all the bodies we left half-buried
in community gardens limbs growing out of the soil with teeth
&nails splaying the roots of oak trees.

We were doomed &I don't think it mattered.
We, in this life,—haunted by others &others
before—could have been strangers perfectly
suited &content to pass each other without notice.

When you told me you didn't deserve me, I should've listened.
Your warning shouldn't have been a challenge.   Or turn-on.
Unfortunately, I am human &when all options are laid out evenly,
I am ready to make poor decisions. Born to die out here in these streets
a crossfire of tar &flames with all the hidden potential of Autumn.

Homecoming
for our Harlem

Returning to our former home was a song to which you never knew the words,
but you mumbled ' til the chorus like a champ.

Each note, was another blue streak, that peeled gravity from air like a tangerine
or another of our arguments.

This feeling was not sinking.
It was, but not really.

It started in my throat and it took everything I had to
force it back down. To swallow this musket ball of a lump.
To add an anchor to that sinking ship.

My chest burned at the weight of it all.
And Langston, and Ella, and Zora, they all watched.
And they all sang. Not really knowing the words. Just faking the funk.

Besides stretch marks, scars, & a muddy set of paws at the front door,
I have nothing to show. Those filthy prints mocked me at my threshold.
They stood turned out like a pretty bird or a young dancer.

When no one was looking, I bent down, dipped my fingertips into the mud
and lifted the brick-sand to my lips. I tasted our dirt—the pith of a shriveled lime
and dirty pennies. Like old blood.

Saudade
for Joseph

means missing as much as absent means
        broken-off at the hilt or unable to forge a sickle
        to protect yourself from the sharpness of yearning.

means missing as much as *How did you get here? Nobody's s'posed to be here!*
means *There's stranger in my house?!*
means *Set me free, why don't you babe!?*

means *I can't*
means *I won't*
means another *Sorry without I Am.*

means missing as much as unrequited means a pleasure
        you suffer, or an illness you enjoy
means your prayers cannot calm, nor can they destroy.

means missing as much as tears can mean joy or pain
        or *I'm still not OK means I wish I never met you*
        or empty means full of as much as without means *I hate not having.*

means tracing a land's borders where time can only be
        measured in distance from one's homeland
        or the margins or the dearly departed.

means missing as much as you playing victim
means winning an argument I didn't know we were having
means *Fuck you for leaving*, but *Fuck you* more for coming back.

Have you got it in you

to end this?
How about
after I cheat
on you with that bitch you hate so much?
How about
with several
bitches and I
still come home
with them on my breath
and I kiss you
and we fight until
you are inside me
as the sun comes up?
How about when
you realized I
picked fights to get you
to feel something?
Did you know
how much I wanted you
to want me?

How about when
I suggested you get
your own life? Your own
friends. Why are you always there
puppy doggin' me? How
about after I gain 50 pounds
and I refuse to admit
I am depressed?

How about when
I said you and that white boy
are spending too much time together?
How about when I said
anybody,
anybody,
but not him?
How about
when you lied?
You agreed. Not him.
Said he wasn't your type and made a face
to prove he wasn't. But I knew.

How about when
I put you in a headlock
and threw your pills across the room
and you never found them
even after you moved to California
with that fucking white boy?

How about after my brother-in-law
filmed you passed out drunk at a party
after throwing up everything you ever ate in your life?

How about when
you didn't wanna touch me anymore because
you didn't love me anymore? Because you found out
all of the shit I did. All of the shit I wanted to do.
How about after I gave you out after out?

You never had the balls
to set me loose.
Not because of me.

Not because of love.
Or the furniture. Or the money.
I think you didn't want to face you.

COLD WAR

A work of art, we were
        innocent. I wish I could
absolve us of everything,
        grant clemency, beg you
pardon, but if you don't let me
        go, we both stay here. Stuck
in a ceasefire that lasts forever
        that is not true peace, but entrapment.
Watching you watching me
        through a scope, crosshaired
and waiting for the other side
        to blink. Or sneeze. Or post
a photo of you and a new me
        smiling on a beach, so that I
might scour the captions for
        something that shows me you
are ready to move on. There
        have been a few new me's.
Mutual friends say *downgrade*
        and other shit that doesn't matter
and some shit that does. Like
        nothing. The nothing means
it's serious. The nothing
        means maybe it has been so many years
that they don't think I even care.
        The difference between
out of and into thin air.
        I'd rather you chose me.

Shelter-in-Place, May 2020.

boys on screens, big at play,

iridescent in leather masks

they come to curl to come to bury (soil) to (swell up) solid to ride

to my locked bed: birdhouse-empty,
chevroned into pipe &shovel(ed) to
leak, to bleed, to speak for Texas
for head to give
for rain

stem & leaf
milk & onion
daub   & wattle
mortise & tenon
chicken   & cob
neighbors & friends

We sink. I
dream. He
binds. He
jerks.

I see. I do.
We here,

be. We here,
did.

We fight. [They]
(our stories) wisp
(Let) [us] live enough
for a poem.

Kissing David, 1994
after Luna Luis Ortiz'

In a cascade of hammers, I ferret around
        for what your voice sounds like.

To hear your name thrashing through the teeth of anyone that knows you
        summons giants and Psalms. I collect each of their stories
and cleave to wonderment.

        What must it have been
                to be so beautiful
                        for your whole life?

I imagine aloud the lines of the rose on your forearm
        while doing the chores you did without me
ever having to ask. The dishes and the way you got more water on you
        than in the sink. I try to hold onto whatever's left of you
that I didn't lose. Or burn. Or chose to forget, but mostly I dance
        to house mixes and hold myself like you would.

To keep me sharp, I grip my own neck
        the way I would yours. I want so much
from our past. I want to replay and remix; to revel in
        black & white. From afar,
I realize you have been beautiful for my whole life.

Or at least for however long I knew of you.
        Staring back at me.
                Thirstily aware that you were love. And by that measure
                                so was I.

Understudy

After another sangria, I finally said it

                                       with someone.

Across from me sat M, his face checkered with stars,
but not stars—tea-lights.

He never told me he was   *with me.*

Perhaps out of respect for my relationship.
Perhaps he was waiting for me to say something.

With is a funny word when it follows

                                         I'm in love

You only want one thing to follow it

                                         with you.

M grabbed my hand.

This was not a vigil. Until it was.

Years ago, after a night so tequila his dimples filled in,
M & I took a cab back uptown. Laying across the backseat
his head in my lap. He smiled up at me. And I fell.
M was a beautiful dancer and when we danced,
his lower lip would skip across mine. A mistake
for which I held my breath that he might make it once more.

                                             And again, he would.

After sangria number whatever, he wondered aloud
                    With whom?

If this were a reality show, we would go to commercial here.

During the break, viewers and superfans would tweet #teamM.
Redditors would bitch about the Ross&Rachelness of it all.

This would only be part one of a two-part cliffhanger
with a two-week break—before the finale.

Coworkers would bicker in bars over PBRs.
Strangers would harumph in waiting rooms. Besties would leave brunch no longer friends.

After much sangria, in many pitchers, I said it

        I'm gonna leave him.

His voice was soft as a wolf in wool.
Like his hand. Like *why not me?*

Soft as *don't go*. Wolf like *you don't have to*.

Soft like you *scare me*. Wolf as in *how could you?*

At a bus stop, I parsed out my men.

Mustachioed false gods—too young and too old.
They were people, not as much as they were objects.
A collection of dickpics and trinkets and tchotchkes;
a not-so-well-curated exhibit. A few were smart, but
usually in ways that made little money and lesser sense.
My very own menagerie of pet peeves in glass, leather, and denim.

A bus pulls up beside a woman in red rain boots and lycra
pulled to sheer black. I follow her lead, watching the sheer
soak her skin with rain when I heard a whimper. Like a kitten
in the distance it eked: you are not coming back. I'd take you. In
a second. Weakness is hubris. Hubris is how it feels to love
someone down to nothing but grey and sky.

I sit beside her and think about men and sin until I give up
my seat for another woman without an umbrella and
the rain sheets the windows and sky so they are both the same.

Hope is a dangerous thing and love is not

an excuse. I am
a feather willing
to forgive everything
if you could
be my pitiful Christ
and I, your Veronica.

I don't know how to
pretend anymore. I have
spent so many mornings
taking wing: faking sleep
and doing things to one-up what I suspect you are doing
and feeling as if I don't, but I care. Oh lord, I care.

As I walk and breathe, grateful to have loved as much as I have lost
I watched you: two men, indistinguishable.
The same way one season is persuaded to become the next.
One inside joke followed by another and it wasn't the men,
it was him. I grit my teeth to migraine at any mention
of him and knew—if I had asked—you would have been too afraid
to tell the truth. So I have been taking in water. Trying to
find new ways to break my beak. Forcing patience down to the cellular level.

Still, I each question simmered long enough to burn
butter. Every imagined answer more veiled and less likely
to form matter. And I take my breaths, shallow like conditional love,
or dust, or pollen whenever I consider you will remember me
less, or worse, you have replaced me.

What would our lives have been if we stayed on that train?

I woke up from that dream, again.
The one that matched the color of
us staying home from work to watch
a whole season of *Ugly Betty* and I turned
to wake you so we could laugh like we did
that day, but you don't live here anymore.

I wonder if that is what life is like on a train.
That yellow &blue bullet from a place that spoke
German with a French accent to one that spoke
French with a German one. We laughed so much then, too.
Mostly from sleep deprivation. Country to country. No clue
the language to butcher.

Do you still wish I came with you? And I'd pick you up from work.
And we'd make pasta together. So much pasta you'd take leftovers
to work the next day and when you came home you'd say, "Babe,
it was so much better today, right?" I'd agree and we would laugh,
but not talk about what was broken. I miss that. Not dealing with

what was not
working was
our perfect.
We were

smart. We both knew what we were doing. We went to good schools.
We *were* smart enough to fix our perfect. But I think we didn't want to.
Maybe we were afraid that if we tried too hard that we'd have nothing to
show for it. Maybe the past is like *that*. Like *don't go*. Like *don't feel you have to*.

Like running far
and so far my ankles
break into a million little lego pieces.
Like the way I used to be.

Glasshaus Girl
after Róisín Murphy

If I had a dime for every time I stood in the middle of a room
in an overcoat over nothing, but bad skin and cruel intentions,
I could buy you a really nice gift.
And I would.
And I'll tell you why.
Because I am a very nice person
who makes very poor—but very nice—decisions.
Which is how I wound up here
standing on the ledge of a fancy hotel
with an Oscar gown's-worth of lace stitched into my pockets
and I am almost not   not crazy   and here's why:

First, there is You. Always you.
>   In a black tux and a leather wig not completely unlike a penguin.

Then, there is me. Usually me.
>   In clip-on earrings made to resemble the Chrysler Building, of course.

Also, there was us. No longer a we, but a you—and a separate I—running
>   lines in a black box living room.
Each time we ran them you'd stir up the clouds and I'd allow you to
>   kiss the veils from my face.

Sometimes I'd call you director, but that's because you picked me
>   up off the floor of yellow-sick, split-felt and spit-ash
all the while walking on tiny eggshells because I am
>   a Creative. A Son of a Gun.

I'd sit there spinning   a hard-boiled egg
      waiting for the equinox   or the answer to who's in charge of this
race, this fiasco, this   boat ride
      ticking side to side on dark waters like a time bomb or Princess Di
sensually eating *that*   aforementioned hard-boiled egg
      with a velvet ring box fascinator full of pills perched atop my head.

Oh, and Little Edie is there, too.
Sorry if I didn't mention that earlier.
And she kisses the entire audience
in one gulp flanked by flowers and candlelight.

At this point, I've lost sight of your face,
but I know I loved every minute of it.

In the Shape of a Girl

Physical voltage, careless and violent. She's slept
beneath city stars since what would have been
her Sweet Sixteen; a gun underneath her pillow.

It is more human to be the girl.
Lucid and soft enough to feel a man's hands
beaten to lace. She's the sudden urge to whisper underwater.
Soft as the algae sitting shiva above the lake, where they found her.

There have been a few
news-cycles since   her
wreckage was pulled
from the nightshade.

When they confused
her pronoun. Treated
her like a prodigal son
guilty of Wednesday.

They etched   'he'
in black cursive,
to cover   her
heart, they called

for   her
in   her
birth name.
Nishanth,
the first half
of a long day.

A brick house
tumbling in velvet
lipstick. Her voice is
almond, Falernum, and one
hundred different kinds of silence.

She speaks in riddles like a fortune cookie
with its paper torn out. A pretty young priss
in patent leather pink Mary Janes, she has eyes like
candied ginger and Meyer lemon zest. Her ponytail
snatched for the gods. Her dress perfectly pressed
pleats and platitudes. She curtsies surreptitiously
for every passerby. She is a body.

Self-Portrait
as a Sycamore

I've planted myself asunder, darkly beneath
       a city of alwayses &hypotheticals. I am

not now, nor shall I ever be a technicolor lotus.
       And that is not for lack of trying. I am

a sycamore, insolent with vertigo and a half-thousand goodbyes.

In Autumn, my itchy bark scabs the pavement
       clumsy as a man shaving against the grain.

In Winter, my hands form three-scaled buds:
       sticky, rank, almost-leaves.

In Spring, I burst violent as dusk.
       Heavy are my blossoms. Heavy as a crown and I stand mighty as I
could tall.

By Summer, I might be a chifforobe
full of nothing, but church-going clothes
for a church-going girl. A nimble flash of
bronze when she sings, or dances, or tells a story,
or whenever she wants to be. A girl who doesn't believe
in anything.

Shelter-in-Place, June 2020

I wake up early.
Draw a bath.
Slather charcoal
across my face.
Set a timer.
Summon
as lavender a sunrise
as I could muster. Steep myself
in rosewater, too hot for skin.

I condition my hair. Deeply.
Coconut & jamaica.
An oil to leave behind.
The time goes off.
I get up and blow dry my
chest and face and hair
until the room smells like
fruit & cream & skin—
summer in Puerto Rico
before the whiteness.

Soft-served as gold
from straw. Spun.
I stare at the bone
-straight hair. Smile.
It sits tame. A stranger

you see often enough
to introduce to your friends & family,
but it's not *like that*.

I go to the track. Run.
I wear no hat. Run.
Mile for mile, run.
I feel the sun
trapped under my skin
dancing that same honey-brown
of generations I will never meet.
I sweat serpents into my eyes
and know I am back to myself.
Salvaje
&Curly
&Brown.

Self-portrait as
Boy in Nail Polish

That boy sweet. Sweet like sugar
should be. Like mango gets. Sweet

so sweet it gets caught between
your teeth. Orange-honey, blossomed.

Syrupy as agave is sweet. Sweet enough
to sugar the red outta some Kool-aid.

That boy got more den a lil' sugar in his tank.
Sweet as   *flowers bloomin', mornin' dew &the beauty seems to say*
                       it's a pleasure when you treasure all that's new&true&

That boy caña stabbed through a mojito
begging to lay in teeth. That boy

folded hands &crossed legs;
don't start none, won't be none

Sugar-pie, honey-bunch! Sweet'r den
rainbow-sprinkle buttercream.

Sweet'r den water ice, or piraguas in July.
That boy sweet'r den a mug o' hot cocoa & cinnamon
           of Marshmallow Fluff Horchata
           of Matcha sweet tea on ice

of Red Velvet Amaretto gelato.

Sweet as lavender caramel madeleines
That boy Nutella whispered on street corner
in Gay-Paris. Maraschino cherries soaked in
Pepsi and candied raspberries after hotboxing
up the coast. Burn your throat, he so sweet.

The Price of Flour

Once upon a pink cotton dhurrie,
Jade Tiger lifted herself and stretched
across the dust to begin her day.

Gathering a few pinches of salt,
a bowl of water, a fist of flour,
and a wink of oil, she enjoyed a kitten's yawn.

Squinting tiny eyes, Jade winked her oil
and pinched her salt, but her fistful of flour
was not enough.

In an eddy, she roared and
smashed every jar and
secret place in her room.

Huffing and puffing upon her dhurrie,
Little Jade cadged the gods for just enough money
to buy just enough flour to make a little bread.

Then it struck her,
          look under the rug!

Counting her treasure only once—and in haste—
she zipped out to the nearest shop with just enough
clinking in the front pocket of her housecoat.

She ran as if scaly reptiles were chasing her.

Something she often did all the while taunting
her monsters. They never caught her. Never would.

When she was close enough to read the shop-sign,
Tiger slowed to her pace to wipe her brow.

She felt her hunger bite through her housecoat.
Tiger smiled as she crossed the threshold and
pounced towards the sacks of flour: atta, sooji, dhal, rice, and so on.

Pawing the largest bag of atta she could, Tiger shuffled
towards the shopkeep. With a thud, she dropped her bag
onto the counter, reached into her pocket,

but there was nothing.

The shopkeep was a tall, grey shadow
older than her father.
He had brown spots stabbed along his cheeks
like scales.

He smiled a dishwater smile. A smile that reminded her of
drain stops and bookshelf dust swept into her lungs.

Tiger stood still.
He let out a sound.

She remembered her monsters.
How they had never caught her. Never would.

The shopkeep licked his chops
not completely unlike a gila monster.

He lowered his palm to rest it on her paw.
The fur on her neck lifted like the gasp did her chest.

She snatched the flour with her bangled paws
and snarled at the lizard-faced shopkeep and
took off taunting like her mother had taught her.

Natalie Wood

I've been looking for my body in the middle of an ocean since
November 29, 1981.

> Lock the bathroom door behind you.
> Take my hand.

My body—which looks like most bodies: creaky &ready to feed creatures
that look like it—has grown weary.

When he's gone, I will | you will walk around with a silver bullet
on my | on your tongue

& when I pull | you pull the trigger, I will find you   stuck
in the middle of last night's mess.

> Let the faucets run.
> Sink &tub. Run.

Running, we are | I am &out of
my mind.

I am | we are hardly the woman I once was | you were
and the same could be said of many women. I am

treading helpless waters   my natural urge to be
swallowed up   in an ocean.

A place to which he might return. An any-ocean.

A place to furl naked, numb &raveled   again.

An ocean full of my flesh,
of foam & song. My *him* was
heavy machinery and I shouldn't | we shouldn't
miss him—deserts &rain—but I am | you are everything, but the girl.

My biggest fear is that I am
Natalie Wood. Unsolved. Murky.
Underneath. A body
under a body   of hydrogen.
of oxygen.   of hydrogen.
And I almost am.
Almost was.

Four tiny wings emblazoned, I've found the body
of a dragonfly among the weeds.
Recklessly, headlessly searching.

        Hand me a bobby pin. Watch me rig this toilet tank.   Like so.
        Bend the pin's legs   into a l o o p ,   this way.
        Prop up the float arm. This will cause the tank to   overflow.

        Are you sure you locked that door?

He's gonna know
        the door's locked.
He's gonna keep
        slamming his shoulders into it.
Left.   Bang.
Then left, again.
Still locked.   Bang.
He's gonna twist

the knob.
The right shoulder.
Tattoo-close, then pause.　　S l i d e .　　　　　　　　Breath.
　　Left, again.　　　Smash, release.

Now I hide　　|　　you hide beneath the sink's skirt
beside a mop-bucket filled with silverfish,　　　　　　　　almost
dead.

　　　　　　　　　　　　Holdyourbreath.
The water is higher than you can breathe.
When the door spills open, the pulp will slurry through.
Borders crossed
　　　　by force
　　　　by man
　　　　by him &fat fingers
　　　　by hips &bones smashing into　　　　and through　　*no*
　　　　　　　　　　　　　　　　　　　　　　　　　　　&please
　　　　　　　　　　　　　　　　　　　　　　　　　　　&stop.

And then, nothing.
No one. Just skin
and barely that.

　　　　Keep your knees bent to your chin. Pull me closer
　　　　Holdyourbreath.
　　　　Fall in.

Close isn't close enough if I feel　　|　　you feel
the cold hit the parts where I am　　|　　you are not. The ocean floor is
a much more fitting end than me　　　shrunk down to what is left
after a man is done.

Mother and Child
after Uemura Shōen,
Mother and Child

Facing the tatami wall hangings, a little yellow moth fusses
in his mother's grip. Little Moth blows bubbles and curls
his tiny tongue to make a lovely clicking song. His mother
stands stiff as an ibis made of wire. Her wings, raw silk
and billowing—a gift from the French set adrift a salty river.

Mother's neck bends to meet her Little Moth.
Under her gaze he gnaws the air, unceasingly. In fact,
he clinks more musically with his budding legs and pointy proboscis like
a secondhand clarinet she'd saved all month for in hopes that
Little Moth would become much more than yellow wings in the glow of a
street lamp.

Portrait of my Mother as Nina Simone

i

Love me, love me. Say you do.
Let me fly away with you.

Mona Lisa set adrift
an obsidian rill—
Vantablack &crystalline—

the king sits bewitched
at the dazzlement
of her piano.

Moon in her breath
trying to find the ocean
looking everywhere

singing to the sidewalk
of stars that come and
go. Static as blackness.

Blackness
bright as
smiling

in the dark.

Don't let him take me. Don't
let him handle me & drive me mad.

Saddidily she trilled
in an antique necklace—
jaguar tooth &bone.

A little girl jostling
fro and to in a pastel blue
claw-foot bathtub

set in the center of a house
in the center of parish
in the center of New Orleans

wishing aloud for the rise of a sun.
Oh, how they hide their faces
as our cities die.

They hide their eyes, too.

Alabama.
Tennessee.
Mississippi. Goddamn.

She ached for us
to let the candles
burn slow. Slow, but hot.

Wool-strong.
Hips &mouth.
Between worlds.

ii

The death of a mother—how symmetrical!
Humdrum as a cemetery herself. She &I both,

museums of skeleton &wire hangers walking
and talking in circles—clock &counter.

To get to know someone as you transform them is selfish.

To take refuge inside a person: the ultimate crime.

My life—silly as it's been
full of user names and oleander—

has infringed upon Her own.
Not just Her body,   Her.

There is no way to know a person before you knew them.

The way they were before you interrupted them.

The way they are with other people. Unfettered. Embarrassing,
Intangibly Her.

My mother had many voices.
The one on the answering machine was my favorite.

It was Her job interview voice—
the one she put on for white people,

you could hear candles melting, the color of
my true love's hair blackening through perfume.

My mother, bless Her heart, had a lot to say
because she was on fire. She always was

like she always was cleaning the house.

For the kitchen, sage & rosemary.
Lavender &mint for the tub.

Our dining table was slick with lemon oil.
And every floor sighed of ammonia &camphor.

She built clouds of cirrus, myrrh, thunder, and coal.
My mother loved a clean that burned.

As a younger man, full of my own clouds,
I hung my head at the burial of my lover's father.

I scanned the stones that jut from the earth like bad teeth
looking for someone I knew. To feel what he was.

I didn't know what it was to lose a parent.
Not that way.

I saw my father's name—my name—
and I felt it.

Everyone talks about life flashing, but it is much worse
to see your death flash before you.

There is no closure. No last hurrah.

No tear-filled wake. No fire, no pyre.

Just loose dirt and stone.

When your mortal coils its last time,
there is no very-special episode moment.

A few stones away, I saw another name—
my mother's.

Her maiden name.
No violins. No piano.

iii

I am sorry.

You never heard that from your mother,
spent forever not saying it, but I'm not sorry for that.

I should end there.

But I can't.
I am your son.

You took my father and made him into three children.
A feat of genius. A celebration of the messes men are.

You taught me a woman's body was not a plot of land for men
to sow whatever they saw fit.

I never asked you about your body.

I am sorry. I'm no different.

I am sorry your body lost a daughter.
I was born of the space she left behind.

We were sisters, then brothers.
two little yins yearning for the world.

She was a beautiful singer. She taught me.
I sing to remember her.

I am sorry I never knew what to ask when you spoke of fibroids.
Photos of child-sized growths you carried with grace to full & fuller term,

living them out.

Your body in a hospital gown was so normal you wore bedsheets around the
house
like Athena, though you were clearly Zeus.

I was so sure I had sprung from your mind
I kissed your forehead whenever I had the chance, out of respect.

We were those gods—Zeus & Athena.
You taught me to question gods at every turn.

I kissed your forehead because it was the only home I never had to pack up
in boxes.

I kissed your forehead as sorry. As thank you. As goodnight. As pretty please.

We moved around so much because of our bodies.

Brown and moving bodies—a language we shared.

I am sorry I never asked about your body when they took it from you.

With all the eyes in the world you asked
I am not a woman anymore?

A statement in a question's body—
the color of scars and so much blood.

I am sorry I never asked you what no one ever asked you.

I'd spend my entire life apologizing for you
as if your body was a place I could pray you out of.

Pietà

Your Honor,

I loved him. Yeah, maybe I coulda' held him longer.
Fed him from my body like an animal,
or dirty hippie, but like I said... I loved him.
Maybe not in your way, but I did.
On my own terms.

Y'know, I caught him once—
my only little boy—
dancing in my purple gown.
The silk one I wore to Nilda's wedding.
The one that ended before the open bar did.

That was a lie. I caught him
more than once. Almost yelled,
but nothing. He looked good in purple.
Was a good dancer, too. Not good.
Great.

I would watch as he sung into my hairbrush
I need you / by me / beside me / to guide me
to hold me / to scold me / 'Cuz when I'm bad
I'm so, so bad...I couldn't not watch, but
I never clapped. That was a lie. I did. Always did.

You ever have that dream where you fix your mouth to scream,
but nada? Silence and nothing but.

I've had mine every night
for so many years
I've lost count.

In my dream, I lost him in a department store.
I know, it isn't evening-newsworthy. It's not
even enough for a Lifetime Movie, but
when it's the first time you lose your son,
it feels like a pretty damned big deal.

In my dream, I couldn't hear myself.
Seems as if no one could.
So I force the silent out until
a salesman runs over to stop me
from snapping sundresses off their racks.

I tried to explain I was dying to the man.

That I was searching for my little boy in corduroy overalls.
He smiled.

And I felt the vessels in my face burst.

Did he hear me?

I grip his collar and silent through him
>   Someone left /my cake out / in the rain
>   I don't   / think that I can take it
>   'cuz it took too long / to bake it
>   I'll never have that recipe again

And we crash into the counter
spilling eau de toilette

and aftershave across the marble.
Security rushes over. Tackles me.
I hear my right leg snap. Then my left.

Fellow-shoppers scurry over
to steal a glimpse
of a glass-freckled
musk-sweet
&sanguine me.

A study of the Vitruvian [wo]man
in red
on marble
lying there
stigmata-still.

Someone fans me with a circular.
Bargain hunting mouths open
morse &blip
silent circles
&dashes.

I swear one cries out
leave her there!
another lower her head!
Or *lift her feet!*
I only hear my pulse, but I swear

I hear them.

I try to explain,
but silence.

Silence stretched wide enough
to catch the dropping of eaves.
That dream's pale compared to the real thing.

In real life, you *do* scream.
And though they hear you,
they won't listen. They refuse.
Won't believe you
when you beg for help.

Or when I say I loved him.

They think I made it up. Him up. Like you do.

Hysterical, like the doctors say.

Maybe they're right.

But all the pieces are here, Your Honor.
These pieces are more than a mother
&her son, more than dwindling search parties,
or national coverage
or my biggest fears.

...but I did.
On my own terms.

Gate 28, Southwest Airlines

...would love to pay for your flight. It would mean so much
to Ellen   and Jack   if you could come.

Yep,   was in her arms when it happened. Life's funny that way.
Well, of course I don't mean funny *that way*,   don't be silly.

Like I said before, I would love to pay for your flight.
This is a time for family.   Your sister needs you.

You'da thought the whole sky fell right on her forehead by the sound
of her. Sight ain't much better, to tell the truth.

Yes, *it is*   last minute.Yes, it *will be*   expensive, but don't you worry about *that*.
I have a little extra saved for days like these.

No, of course I didn't think *this* would happen to Ellen. Even though
she told people too soon. And bought too many toys before she was outta the woods.

But I don't blame her   or Jack   for this.
Who could?

I know, that's precisely what I'm saying. Mysterious ways, and...ok,
ok, let's not   bring Him   into this.

Hey, I saw those photos you put up on the Internet,
I don't think I ever saw *that* dress.

Y'know, I always admired your eye for patterns and colors.
So free. I could never wear such wonderfully busy clothing.

You must come, sweetie. I know, but all *that* is water under the bridge.
I am sure Ellen has forgiven you by now.   Oh,

I'm sorry, then *you* oughta get over it. This is not the time
to talk about genders and *hes* or *shes* or *theys* or *its*. I love you. Just come.

there is no more blue
Francisco to his daughter

The sky is collapsing, but his stars are lucky.
You sat beside me in a room like this one
and forgave me. My youngest daughter,
you are a web of stardust and frequencies
that document the fall of Man.
A newly-constructed constellation.
Be still for me.
Do not cry for this vessel.
Do not mourn its old skin.
For now, I am Winter and all it entails.

Do not worry about where I will go.
I have made amends for my filth,
my twelve-hundred months of silt.
I will be where I will be.

Before I left you, I squinted
so tightly I recalled the first colours
of your first days and suddenly the air was blue.
Blue like the quiet there was when you became light.
A light, blue enough, to swallow us whole.
A cold light to be caught in the wind and never again,
but on that final night I slowly pulled the light in
with both my fists,
two trembling pebbles
wishing to be stones.

I left you the stars as they fell
to scatter like newly-freed horses
so that we—two halves of one story—
could perchance collide tomorrow
in song and shelter.

My youngest daughter, skin of Spring
and Summer and recent Autumn,
my greatest hope is that you escape
the absence that awaits before you, too,
are old skin and Winter.

Room 31B

A hospital's a shitty place to die
and an even shittier place to live.

Every Tuesday afternoon, anchors shredded my ankles,
and I tore up the linoleum on the plank-walk to room 31B.

I hated visiting.

His room always smelled like used tongue depressors, disinfectant, and dirty gauze.
Every surface crawled with amoebas dancing to the squiggle of meal-cart wheels.

Even the Sun refused to stream past the brick-view outside his beige-paneled window.

I cannot remember that man before there was a room 31B.
I want to believe he was once a man. A great one. I cannot be sure.

In his bed, he slept between bars like a wet rodent in a cage.
He had a pirate map for a face. One covered in dead ant segments.
One that lit up for the wobble of green jello on pink dishwasher-warped trays.

Whenever his family visited, they stood cursed and firm like pillars of salt.
Twisted and gnarled necks, hunting for a clock to absolve them.

Each of their puffy faces rhymed like lyrics, swelling from youngest girl
to his eldest son. Their bodies wriggled distances further than futures to bask
and sway in the final flicker of a man. Their arms like vines, their eyes
focused on the machine beside him.

After a spoonful of weeks, the family thinned.

Every mylar well wish ribbon bobbed; each petal no longer velvet.
Victims to shifts in gravity. Or time. Or space.

But most of all, I will not forget the hum and prayer of a wife
unconvincing herself she was too young to widow.

In a voice she saved for the last day—
          a voice she saved for him to hear alone—
she spoke braille into her husband's palm, Go.

Carrier

For him, I never wash my hands. I don't want to
lose any part of him. He'd never seen snow before,
wore his brown leather chanclas, rain or shine.

He taught my bones to love him with his two hands—
two times bigger than mine—he tore ventricles from
chambers &shaped me into a flightless bird.

Laying there nearly conscious, he crossed my threshold.
My San Andreas, a hairline, a line of fault pushed apart.
He promised me Orion's belt and at night—lasso in hand,

elastic around my ankles—he delivered a message on broken latex.
My wings pointlessly outstretched as those gilded palms, I lept
like the boys in Old San Juan off a bridge into the area rocosa.

conversion

a trash compactor in a lab-coat sits
across from us in a small beige

room. he pulls off his glasses. speaks
softly. too softly. takes no breath. no

pause. looks neither of us
in the eye.

Boyfriend grabs my wrist
and vertigo

inside each lung
blackness pools

our chests knotted
and knitted-purls

quicksand blacker than
the breaths we take in.

Boyfriend chokes back sobs thick as chicken fat
in Momma's good skillet.

this thickness throbs
behind his eyes,

too heavy to
hold itself up,

Boyfriend rests His head
in my lap.

M y j o i n t s a c h e,
He says.

I make him strange promises
in beige rooms.

I will fill my veins,
with tenses I am too scared to read aloud.

I will bathe him in salts,
plum-milk and lavender,

f o u r t i m e s a d a y.
His s k i n w i l l g r o w

i r i d e s c e n t for want of
the sun.

one day it will burn
much too much

to speak
of Him.

Living With

Motherfuckin' motherfuckers! I know,
redundant. I also know you're gonna
unsheathe your fine-tipped sharpies
from their Moleskine prisons
and scrape across that first-line,
to make a suggestion for a subtler,
less violent opener, but before you
expose your bias for color, language
and glaring emotion know this:
this is about something. No,
it is not about suffering, or
surviving, or the fears of others.
It is
about the moment
you hover above yourself
as two men rip you apart
artichoke heart
and thistle.
It is
about the gowned moment
you pace—backless—in an office
only sitting once a woman enters,
and insists.
It is
sitting still, besides stuttering
knees jabbing towards a white woman
with the bluest eyes you have ever seen.
It is

not about her
social-worker-voice
telling you a story
about a future where you will
not have to worry about hard-to-swallow,
before bed, once-a-day, empty stomach,
much-too-vivid dreams and bile dawn-flowers
bursting you open. You are not alone.
You are in good company:
Louima. Lucretia. Sakia. Teena.
It is
not about men
who got off after getting off. Those wimps
took what was never theirs and gave us
the right to proclaim:
Motherfuckin' motherfuckers!
Twice in one poem.

Self-Portrait as a Rizzo

Bathed blue-as-mitchell on a summer soft, close enough
to name each pixel I sat crosslegged in my aunt's living room
a mirrored surface|reflecting another close enough to become
Betty Rizzo pondering the polemical pulchritude
of a Miss Patty Simcox and her campaign for Carnival Queen.

With a wispy-thwack, three towheaded teens
and a wanton brunette fluttered-by.
Breathless as they were fervid,
the most flaxen of the four tittered
"That's the one I was *telling you* about."

I always thought Rizzo shoulda' won Grease.
I know. You don't think Grease is a game,
You think it's a musical about greasers &teen sex
&doing whatever it takes to satisfy a villain-hot,
dimple-chinned, leather-clad, lying piece of scum
with an ass that wouldn't know quitting from a can of paint.
       And you don't think that's winnable?
Grease most certainly was a competition.
It—and everything else—always is.

Even before I did anything Rizzo-worthy, I knew I was her,
not like her, *was her*: lithe and sanguine amid daisies
a Babylon Red Dinner Plate Dahlia proselytizing
there are worse things   *I could do*,
a dove's worth of feathers dipped in ink &gripped—pinky, thumb, &ring.
I might've been a-tisket. I was certainly a-tasket, but I wasn't Sandy.
Not silky, nor pastel. Not lousy with V, Sandra Dee. Nosiree, Bob!

but I'll be damned. Damned for sure. Damned for asking anything of
congregations. Damned for lacking the patience to wait
a   few   more   beats to
go with a boy,   *or two.*
Damned to live amber-trapped in this *this*.
Oh, the Rydell-ness of it all. Sick of it I was
Damned to be, but a falling leaf.
A party   girl, on burnt sugar.
A ramekin being used as an ashtray.
An aubergine, skinned. A wind, wild
& wondering why I keep on
&forward &running &keepin' on
counting keeps. Piles &heaps,
bounds & leaps of `em

Even tho' the neighborhood
         Thinks I'm trashy & no good
                  I suppose it could be true
So I sit   &so do you—close as lightning
         sits with thunder.
Close as the choir &Aretha sit cozy with Jesus
         &Jesus does Prince &Prince did Aretha.
Closer than Jesus to Mary, weeping
         or Martha, her mourning.
Closer than the Pharaoh's Army&The Red Sea
         or I do myself when I say,"*Rizzo,*   *don't you weep.*
                                                      Rizzo,   *don't you*

mourn.

Lamb's Ear

Jill tore an ear from a field of shiny blackness. It fit small and innocent in my hand. Immediately, I took the ear and placed it on my tongue just as I was taught by catechists. Before the mastication of a Lamb's Ear, there are several senses one must address: In hand, the ear is soft as one might expect severed cartilage to be. It is fuzzy in a way a kiwi wished it were. Softly, but not meekly. At the center of a palm, the ear is silver-green silk, smooth as Sarah Vaughan covering Ella. To the nose, the Ear's scalloping ekes out a dullen hiss like any other chlorophylled creature— see spider plant or foxglove— but back to the Eucharist, the moment mouth&teeth& littleLamb&latticework roll about. In the mouth, theEarisanunpronounceablecarpaccio. And its texture is cream with a bit more give. Subtle as a bonfire. Subtle as a wound. Subtle enough to remind me of you.

In response to an old white woman saying "I guess we're on Puerto Rican Time"

Say it to my face, so I can spit a jungle down your throat.

Say it so I can hear you say it.

Say it 'til you choke.

Say it so I can interrupt you con una canción Yoruba
so devastatingly brown time itself is recalibrated to
match the clave of Yemaya's footsteps. A song I can dance to—
all hips and ass. Una baila Taino so indigenous you can taste the moment we made the
    Earth.

Ecuo / yalé / yarun mawó / yalé / omi aché aya ma-o mi-o

You say "Puerto Rican Time" like it's a bad thing.
You're late, bitch, no matter when you arrive.

You think 'cuz your daddy came from the Bronx, we cool?
My Bronx is what your papí left behind.
After the fires.
After he reached in and tore my cousins from my Tía's.
After he forced them back to work in the factories he owned.

You ain't no kin to me.

I come from a people stronger than water,
&you're not half the Huracán esa puta María was.

Puerca-traga-sangre-maldita-asquerosa-huele-bicho.

I bet you think this poem's about you.
This is not a poem.
It's an incantation
for my mother
&her tongue
&the many before her
that split time open like a concha freeing the salt-sweet flesh so we might feed.

Esto no es una poema.
This is a cocotazo grandissimo.
Knuckles rapping
at the top of your skull.

Now, *you* are that concha.

De la Lengua

No two are alike
        some, so dissimilar
        they bifurcate the tongue
but it does not break.

To break a tongue
        you must taste it,
        fill your mouth
with the tough and tender of another.

Let their veins wrangle,
        round &roll
        with yours
one muscle conquered by another.

To break a tongue is to explore bodies,
        lands, artifice, ideas of which that tongue obsesses.
        Obsessions expose a tongue's utility.
When a tongue has hundreds of words for something, therein lies a clue.

A former lover told me Eskimos have hundreds of words for snow
        for falling, for fallen, for wet & for dry,
        for slush & for slurry,
but even in the afterglow I knew that was not true.

To break a tongue, you must push past the teeth
        deeper than the flick and sway of muscle and spit.
        Diving into that which the speakers hold dear,
where *why* and *often* intersect. For example:

Shona-speaking people in Zimbabwe have many words for walking.

walking: through mud while making squelching sounds;   *chakwair.*

walking: for a great stretch of time with bare feet;   *dowor.*

walking: huddled together, cold & wet;   *svavair.*

walking: with hips that swing and sway;   *minair.*

walking: in a short, very-short dress;   *pushuk.*

walking: naked;   *shwitair.*

walking: with flesh rippling as a lake;   *seser.*

walking: with thighs so thin you appear to be leaping

—like a grasshopper—rather than walking.   *tabvuk.*

Persians have a word for looking beautiful
after a disease   *mahj.*

In Cameroon, they've a Bakweri word for
when children smile in their sleep   *wo-mba.*

Indonesians have a word for the moments in which one is
so grief-stricken they are unable to make a decision   *termangu-mangu.*

There were many words for what I was
in Spanish.
Insects and
winged-insults.

There are still many words for what I am
in Spanish.
Few of them made me
proud. Butterflies and Ducks.

There are many more for what little boys and little girls are
in Spanish.

Many of them less than
human; dirty and
animal. Sticks, and
stones, and so on.

To break a tongue, you must fill your mouth   *choke.*

reading guide

Theme: **The Perception of Failure | Success**

Many of the poems in Like Sugar dissect the concept of failure. The speakers exist in a world where, in order to understand failure, one must concede that its counterpart, "success," is not static. In the collection's opening poem, "domestic," failure is defined in a very bold way. Does this definition align with your own? How does this articulation of failure set a tone for the rest of the collection?

The fear of failure/success can be debilitating. While reading this collection look for examples of lines, images, word choices, and speakers that seek to utilize that fear as motivation. [not sure what "utilize fear as a motivation" means. Let me think about another phrasing.]

Representative Poems
that illustrate the impact of failure are:
- "domestic" (pp. 1)
- "Security is a Cockroach" (pp. 3)
- "mother" (pp. 97)

Prompt:

Think about a time when you failed. This could be a moment when you failed a test, or when you failed to speak up on your own behalf or perhaps for another person/group. Perhaps it is a moment where you failed to apologize, or maybe it is a part of your past that you failed to relinquish.

Write about this moment/these moments from the perspective of some people gossiping about their mutual friend(s). Pick a place that could be full of overheard conversations to find a title.

Theme: **A Sense of Urgency**

Many of the poems in *Like Sugar* directly address another person in order to convey a message they were not able to convey in an earlier time. How does time pass in the collection? How does the collection's sense of time shape the urgency of its speakers' desires? Does time pass uniformly in this collection or are there moments of transition, compression, and trancendence of time? What is the collection's relationship to the changing of seasons?

Representative Poems
Some examples of poems that illustrate the passage of time are:
- "Self-Portrait as a Sycamore" (pp. 86)
- "there is no more blue." (pp. 111)
- "Room 31B " (pp. 113)

Prompt:

What is one lesson about yourself/family you wish you would have learned sooner? Write from the perspective of someone that goes to extremes to teach you this lesson repeatedly.

Look up some "famous last words." Write a poem that refutes these words for very personal reasons disguised as selfless advice.

Theme: **The Role of Violence**

Like Sugar examines the tumultuous relationship between love and anger in a variety of ways. Sometimes that relationship is built on wildness and passion; in other moments it is violent and destructive. Some of the speakers come to realize what they once thought to be passion is no longer that, but something far more sinister. What role does consent play in the collection? Which poems might present similar accounts of consent, passion, and violence? Which might offer differing views? What role does rage play in this collection? How does ownership (of pain/rage/fear/desire) manifest itself in these poems?

Representative Poems
Some examples of poems that illustrate ownership of violence and passion are:
- "all my life..." (pp. 34)
- "...Puerto Rican Time" (pp. 123)
- "Watch Me Catch Fire..." (pp. 15)

Prompt:

Select one of the aforementioned poems and write from the perspective of the person/persons addressed in the poem. Try to write your first draft in a 5 minute uninterrupted freewrite. Let the emotions take the lead and go big with each line. Once the first draft is done, set the draft aside for a few days. When you revisit the draft, pay particular attention to the reasons your speaker responded and make sure the verbs you keep in the next draft are evocative and explicit. Consider your speaker and why they are responding to the poem you selected. Are they responding in order to share their side? To apologize? To shout into the void?

acknowledgments

So many people helped to make this collection possible and I hope that I will one day be worthy of your time and love and lives. I am going to try to celebrate some of the people that reminded me that I am forever on the guest list and sitting pretty in the VIP.

For my mother. You are my drag inspiration. Mother of the Haus. My success—large or small—is a testament to how phenomenally-magical Puerto Rican women from the projects in the Bronx are! This collection would not exist without you. You taught me to celebrate the things about myself that others mock. You taught me to "never stay hit from NO ONE." And something I remind myself everyday, "you don't have no hairs your tongue." As a queer person of color, social worker, poet, & whatever comes next I pledge to use my voice to make change for future generations.

For Dad. I love you. I hope you understand that I appreciate and celebrate you for trying. I am so proud of you. I hope we both get to introduce one another to the men we are becoming. I am ready to go fishing when you are.

For Jenn. I miss you always. I am not sure you know how much being your big brother means to me. I am proud of you for always being you. You made me all the more me. If you and I don't hangout before the next collection comes out...I will be writing a dis-record and the remix WILL feature Sailor Moon.

For Chris. I love you. Even though you would steal my Jordan's, scuff them up, and place them back in my closet. Hope to get to know you as the father, husband, hero, and man you are and not the boy you were.

For Ryan & Lucas, I am so happy to have you boys in my life. Watching you grow up has been such a joyful experience. If you ever need anything, Uncle Suki got you! (ummm...there are some poems in this collection that I will have to explain when you are older. MUCH older.)

For Marilyn & Dick. Thank you for showing me that family can grow. And for laughter, love, mango vodka duty, and caviar on potato chips!

For Miguel, Vlad, Jonathan, Erick, James, Bobby, George, Angelo, PCII, Joaquín, Juan, Kyle, Marcos, Freddy, Sergio, Eddie, Juli, Baruch, Luis, Dino, Noris, Lorenzo, Bry, Kazim, Paul, Sam, Marcelo, Josh, Lun, Stephen, and all the queerdos that have kiki'd with me way past our bedtimes on school nights, let's do it again sometime.

For Marina, Aaron Michael, Dana, Bryanna, Mike, & Jon.

For Brenda Shaughnessy. Reading with you is a privilege. Being your friend is an honor.

For Rachel Hadas. I hope to one day be half as cool as you.

For Rigoberto Gonzalez. The fairy godmother in my mind!

For Emanuel Xavier. I am forever your fan. Thank you for every word.

For Cindy Cruz. You took me seriously as an undergrad poet. Thank you forever.

For Cathy Park Hong. You pushed me in an undergrad workshop so hard I decided to get my MFA at the end of the course. Thank you for always.

For Diane Seuss. I am sure you already know, but you are an inspiration to me. You taught me to "fog the stars beautiful" and I ain't never going back!

For my UC BerkeleyMSWfam: ROX, HAEWON, SYLVIA, SARA, MISH, SYLVIA, KENDRA, NOOR, MIKE, OMAR, LUNA, EVELYN, and every single person I stayed up late night writing papers and finishing projects seconds before deadlines with at Cal! Being a Commencement speaker for the UC Berkeley MSW Class of `19 was more than a lil' brown boy was supposed to dream about...we should them! And my nephews got to watch me do it, so they know now that not only is it possible, but it runs in the family!

For Pabz! The thing about losing the "love of your life" is it is a gift if you choose to receive it as such. I know that love is always plural. We will have many. And many more. Thank you for sitting in a park in Montréal with me, a few beers, a few teary apologies, and forgiveness.

For the Nomadic Press family who worked tirelessly with me to turn my thoughts into an artifact: J. K., Michaela. For Natasha. Working with you was silly and serious. I felt loved in our conversations. I can't wait to celebrate in PERSON!

For all the places that accepted and published poems in this collection. For Indolent Books, RADAR, *Ninth Letter*, *The Acentos Review*, Bay Area Generations, Quiet Lightning, *Apogee*, *Anomaly*. Special shoutout to CantoMundo, Vermont Studio Center, Sarah Lawrence College Summer Seminar, Lambda Literary Foundation fellowship, UC Berkeley Center of Excellence, PACE University, and Community of Writers. Through your support, this book is a reality!

ROBERTO F. SANTIAGO

Roberto F. Santiago received an MSW from UC Berkeley and MFA from Rutgers University. His work has appeared in *Apogee, Anomaly, Ninth Letter*, and *The Acentos Review*. Roberto was awarded the Alfred C. Carey Prize and has received fellowships from the Vermont Studio Center, CantoMundo, Community of Writers, Sarah Lawrence College, and the Lambda Literary Foundation. His debut collection, *Angel Park* (2015), appeared on the LA Times list of 23 *Essential New Books by Latino Poets,* and was a finalist for a Lambda Literary Award. Roberto lives in San Francisco, where he works as a social worker and Editor-in-Chief of Sancocho Press, a queer and trans AfroLatinx imprint with Kórima Press. His debut album "Bu$$yCat" is now streaming on all major platforms.

cover missive

On "Hatching Cal" (as part of Staying Positive series)

by artist Alexander Hernandez

Staying Positive started as a series of textile portraits investigating the identities of people of color living with HIV. I used fabrics, patterns, motifs, colors, and imagery showcasing each person's cultural and social background to demonstrate how they navigate their POZ identity as a means of survival throughout their various communities. This show was aimed to dismantle the social stigmas of being positive and showcases this community as survivors rather than victims. It was supposed to go up on May 29, 2020, as part of the Queer Cultural Festival but was postponed indefinitely due to the pandemic. During this whole ordeal, I started making changes to my pieces to reflect the POZ community's commitment to staying healthy. By adding magical animal limbs and other body parts, I transformed my subjects into chimeras. They evolved into fantastical creatures enabling them to adapt to change and chaos. This piece titled "Hatching Cal" is a portrait of Denver based artist Cal Duran, a long-time friend of Hernandez. Duran is shown being reborn through a fabric cocoon that has both smothered him yet kept him warm. Displaying how POZ folks persevere with all the luggage they have to carry.

hernalex.com

OTHER WAYS TO SUPPORT NOMADIC PRESS' WRITERS

In 2020, two funds geared specifically toward supporting our writers were created: the **Nomadic Press Black Writers Fund** and the **Nomadic Press Emergency Fund**.

The former is a forever fund that puts money directly into the pockets of our Black writers. The latter provides dignity-centered emergency grants to any of our writers in need.

Please consider supporting these funds. You can also more generally support Nomadic Press by donating to our general fund via nomadicpress.org/donate and by continuing to buy our books. As always, thank you for your support!

Scan below for more information and/or to donate.
You can also donate at nomadicpress.org/store.